CLASSIC RECIPES

Meals in minutes

simple
and
delicious
food

Wendy Hobson

ARCTURUS

ARCTURUS

This edition published in 2013 by Arcturus Publishing Limited
26/27 Bickels Yard, 151–153 Bermondsey Street,
London SE1 3HA

Copyright © 2013 Arcturus Publishing Limited

All rights reserved. No part of this publication may be reproduced,
stored in a retrieval system, or transmitted, in any form or by
any means, electronic, mechanical, photocopying, recording or
otherwise, without prior written permission in accordance with the
provisions of the Copyright Act 1956 (as amended). Any person or
persons who do any unauthorised act in relation to this publication
may be liable to criminal prosecution and civil claims for damages.

ISBN: 978-1-78212-013-1
AD002585US

Printed in China

Contents

Introduction

There's work, children, parents, families, household chores, shopping, more work . . . the list goes on and on. Every time we invest in another labor-saving device, it seems to create a different kind of work rather than doing away with tasks altogether.

And that applies to our cooking and eating habits too. As we try to cram more and more into our diaries, food often takes a back seat. We grab a ready meal or call for a take-out far more often than is good for us.

It's pointless looking back to days when everything was slower and more leisurely and people had stacks of time on their hands—anyway, most of it is a nostalgic myth! Just look at it from a food perspective. There were no fridges, so you had to shop every day. Freezers—are you kidding me? Spice mixes? Food processors? Exotic ingredients at the local store? None of the above! Would you rather go back? I don't think so.

So let's be realistic and just take what was good about how they used to cook a generation or more ago, then add it to what's great about cooking now. Surely the single most important word is 'fresh': they cooked from scratch with fresh ingredients, usually local. That's a much healthier way of eating—and we all know that— but somehow there's just not the time!

Well, here's a helping hand to introduce you to a collection of tasty dishes that are easy and nutritious—and quick. They use all the modern options, from canned tomatoes to food processors, while bringing you back from the ready-meal brink to good home cooking.

And the key? KISS! Keep It Simple, Stupid! The old marketing expression is as true here as it is elsewhere. Doing something simply and doing it well is far better than overcomplicating the issue—and quicker, too.

So the first thing to do is look in your food cupboard and see what's lurking in there. If it is way past its sell-by date, chuck it out. If you can't remember why you ever bought it, give it away. Now sort out what you have and buy one or two more things when you are at the store so you will always be able to rustle up a simple but tasty meal in minutes. You might keep:

- Canned tomatoes, canned garbanzos or other pulses, tuna or crabmeat.
- Oil, salt and pepper, a few spices and herbs, stock cubes, perhaps a jar of pesto.
- Flour, sugar, pasta, rice, couscous.
- Onions, garlic.

Once your store is in place, you can pick up fresh meat, fish, fruit, and veg as and when you need them. But even without any extras, you could still make a tasty herb risotto, crab pancakes, or a tuna pasta in tomato sauce from your storecupboard—all in minutes!

All you need to do is be determined to find straightforward ways to keep your cooking simple, fresh, and imaginative and you are on your way to enjoying better food, more quickly. And what are you going to do with the time you save? My suggestion would be set the table, pour yourself a glass of something nice (it could be wine or beer but it could equally well be iced water), sit down and really enjoy your meal. Don't rush it, don't eat it on the run—really savor the food and the time you have with your family or friends to talk, to chill out and relax. This is your time to enjoy. Because, after all, you put together the meal in minutes!

Spaghetti carbonara

You can't beat this classic Italian dish when you want to serve a tasty but quick and easy dish after a long day at work. It takes only minutes to prepare from the simplest ingredients but it tastes great.

Serves 4

350g/12oz spaghetti
Salt and freshly ground black pepper
1 tbsp oil
15g/½oz/1 tbsp butter
4 bacon slices, diced
2 garlic cloves, chopped
2 egg yolks
2 eggs
4 tbsp heavy cream
50g/2oz/½ cup freshly grated Parmesan cheese
A few sage leaves

1. Bring a large pan of salted water to the boil, add the spaghetti and boil for about 8 minutes until al dente. Bite a piece – it should be tender but not soggy.
2. Meanwhile, heat the oil and butter in a large pan and sauté the bacon and garlic over a low heat for a few minutes until the bacon is cooked.
3. Mix the egg yolks, eggs, and cream together in a jug and season with salt and pepper.
4. Once the spaghetti is tender, drain it thoroughly, then toss it into the hot pan with the bacon and pour in the eggs and cream. Remove from the heat, add half the Parmesan and toss everything together well. The egg will cook sufficiently in the residual heat.
5. Sprinkle with the remaining Parmesan, garnish with sage and serve at once.

Pepper and tomato bruschetta

Served as an appetizer or a snack, this brightly colored dish combines juicy tomatoes with olives on top of slices of crunchy bread. You can serve the bruschetta with a bowl of fresh salad if you like.

Serves 4

1 small ciabatta or baguette
4 tbsp extra virgin olive oil
4 garlic cloves, halved
8 olives, pitted and sliced
4–6 tomatoes, chopped
Salt and freshly ground black and red peppercorns
50g/2oz/½ cup grated Pecorino cheese
A few basil sprigs

To serve
A few cherry tomatoes
Olive oil and balsamic vinegar (optional)

1. Cut the bread into thick slices. Drizzle with a little of the olive oil and broil until crisp. Rub the cut garlic into the bread.
2. Pile the olives on top, then cover completely with the tomatoes and season sparingly with salt and generously with black and red pepper. Sprinkle with the cheese and garnish with basil.
3. Serve with cherry tomatoes, and some olive oil and balsamic vinegar for sprinkling or dipping, if you like.

Vegetable soup with cheese croûtons

Serves 4

1 tbsp oil

15g/½oz/1 tbsp butter

1 onion, chopped

1 garlic clove, chopped

1 carrot, chopped

1 celery stick, chopped

1 red or green bell pepper, chopped

400g/14oz/1 large can chopped tomatoes

1 litre/1¾pt/4¼ cups vegetable or chicken stock

225g/8oz mixed vegetables of your choice, diced or sliced

Salt and freshly ground black pepper

100g/4oz/1 cup grated Monterey Jack cheese

4 slices of French bread

Flatleaf parsley, to garnish

Full of healthy vegetables, with the extra depth of flavor from the tomatoes, this delicious and rich soup is made more filling with the addition of a cheese toast to soak up the tasty stock.

1. Heat the oil and butter in a large pan and sauté the onion, garlic, carrot, and celery over a low heat for about 5 minutes until soft but not browned.
2. Add the tomatoes and stock and bring to the boil.
3. Add the sliced or diced vegetables, keeping back any that cook quickly to add later so they are all cooked at the same time. Season with salt and pepper and leave to simmer for about 20 minutes until the vegetables are tender and the soup has thickened slightly.
4. Meanwhile, sprinkle the cheese on the bread slices and put under a hot broiler for about 5 minutes until the cheese is hot and melting.
5. Float the bread in the soup, season with salt and pepper, and garnish with parsley to serve.

Serves 4

300g/10oz fusilli (pasta spirals)
Salt and freshly ground black pepper
100g/4oz black olives, pitted
225g/8oz cherry tomatoes, halved
1 red onion, sliced into rings
250g/9oz feta cheese, cut into cubes
2 tbsp chopped mint

For the dressing

100ml/4fl oz/scant ½ cup extra
virgin olive oil
Grated zest and juice of 1 large lemon
1 tbsp wholegrain mustard
2 garlic cloves, crushed

Pasta salad with feta, tomatoes, and olives

Pasta is such a useful standby and makes the basis of this vibrant and colorful salad. Twists of fusilli are used here, but you can substitute any type of pasta you prefer. Vary the ingredients, too, to suit what you have available.

1. Bring a large pan of salted water to the boil, add the pasta and boil for about 8 minutes until just tender but not soggy—test it by trying a piece. Drain and leave to cool.
2. When cool, put the pasta in a bowl and add all the salad ingredients. Toss together carefully so everything is well blended.
3. Whisk together the dressing ingredients. Pour over the salad as you are about to serve and toss together.

Onion and cheese eggplant

Finished with melted cheese, these eggplant shells are topped with a filling mixture of ground beef cooked with onions, tomatoes and peppers. To speed up the recipe, use red bell peppers from a jar. Serve on a bed of rice with a fresh salad.

Serves 4

2 red bell peppers
2 tbsp oil
1 onion, chopped
1 garlic clove, chopped
300g/12oz ground beef
4 eggplants, halved lengthways
250g/9oz/1 cup sieved tomatoes
Salt and freshly ground black pepper
A few basil sprigs
100g/4oz/1 cup freshly grated Parmesan

To serve
Boiled long-grain rice
Salad

1. Heat the broiler. Rub the peppers with a little of the oil and broil until the skin blisters, turning regularly. Place in a plastic bag, tie loosely and leave until cool enough to handle.
2. Heat the remaining oil in a large pan and sauté the onion and garlic for a few minutes until soft but not browned.
3. Add the beef and sauté, stirring, until browned.
4. While it is cooking, scoop the flesh out of the eggplant shells and chop it. Remove the peppers from the bag and run them under a cold tap, stripping off the skin. Dice the flesh.
5. When the beef is browned, add the eggplant to the pan with the sieved tomatoes and peppers. Season with salt and pepper. Chop a few basil leaves and stir them into the pan with the cheese.
6. Spoon the mixture back into the eggplant shells and broil for about 4 minutes until heated through.
7. Sprinkle with the remaining cheese, garnish with basil sprigs and serve with rice and salad.

A selection of colorful vegetables makes this an attractive dish—and it doesn't disappoint in flavor either! Toasting the couscous and soaking it in a tasty stock gives it extra flavor and makes it delicious served either hot or cold.

Serves 4

400g/14oz/2 cups couscous
600ml/1pt/2½ cups hot vegetable stock
2 tbsp oil
2 scallions, chopped
1 garlic clove, crushed
1 red bell pepper, diced
1 yellow bell pepper, diced
8 asparagus spears, cut into chunks
2–3 tbsp pesto sauce
Salt and freshly ground black pepper
8 cherry tomatoes, halved
5cm/2in piece of cucumber, diced
A few basil leaves

Couscous with Mediterranean vegetables

1. Put the couscous in a dry pan and shake over a medium heat for about 3–4 minutes until it turns golden brown. Once it starts to color, remove from the heat and keep shaking the pan so the couscous is golden but not burnt.
2. Pour the hot stock over the couscous so that it comes just above the level of the grain. Stir well, then leave to stand, stirring occasionally so the stock is absorbed evenly.
3. Heat the oil over a medium heat and sauté the scallions, garlic and peppers for about 5 minutes until soft but not browned. Add the asparagus and toss together in the flavored oil. Remove from the heat.
4. Stir the vegetables into the couscous with the pesto sauce and season to taste with salt and pepper, if necessary. Leave to cool.
5. Stir in the tomatoes and cucumber, check and adjust the seasoning to taste and serve garnished with basil leaves.

Mushroom and bacon risotto

The great thing about risotto is that once you know the principles, you can apply them to making any risotto you like, using your favorite ingredients. Use arborio or another medium-grain rice to give a creamy result.

Serves 4

1 tbsp oil

250g/9oz bacon slices, rinded and chopped

1 onion, chopped

2 garlic cloves, crushed

1 tsp thyme leaves

400g/14oz/2 cups arborio rice

3 tbsp white wine

750ml/1¼pts/3 cups hot vegetable stock

1 tbsp pesto sauce

75g/3oz/¾ cup freshly grated Parmesan cheese

Salt and freshly ground black pepper

2 tbsp crème fraîche (optional)

A little chopped parsley

1. Heat the oil in a large skillet and sauté the bacon, onion, and garlic over a medium heat until the onion is tender and the bacon is cooked and beginning to crisp.
2. Add the thyme and stir well, then add the rice and stir until all the grains are coated in the hot oil.
3. Add the wine and stir into the rice for 2 minutes.
4. Begin to add the hot stock a little at a time, stirring continuously, and waiting for the rice to absorb the stock before adding more. Continue until the rice is just tender but not soggy—try a few grains to test if it is ready. It will take about 20 minutes.
5. Stir in the pesto and half the Parmesan, then season to taste with salt and pepper. Remove from the heat. Stir in the crème fraîche if you like a creamier risotto, cover, and keep the risotto warm for 5 minutes to mature the flavors. Serve sprinkled with the remaining parsley and the Parmesan cheese.

Quick potato and garbanzo curry

Serves 4

2 tbsp oil

1 onion, chopped

1 garlic clove, chopped

2 carrots, very finely diced

4 potatoes, peeled and diced

1 tsp turmeric

1 tsp ground cumin

1 tsp chili powder (or to taste)

400g/14oz/1 large can garbanzos, drained

300ml/½pt/1¼ cups chopped tomatoes

200ml/7fl oz/scant 1 cup vegetable stock

Salt and freshly ground black pepper

350g/12oz/1¾ cups long-grain and wild rice mix

Basil sprigs for garnish

To serve

Naan bread

Mango chutney (optional)

Curries are perfect for cold winter evenings but often take a long time to cook. Here's a creamy curry that is also quick and easy to make— ideal for those who want meals in minutes. For a quicker result, use ordinary long-grain rice.

1. Heat the oil and sauté the onion, garlic, and carrots over a low heat for 5 minutes until soft but not browned.
2. Add the potatoes and sauté until just beginning to color.
3. Stir in the spices, adding more or less to suit your own taste, and cook for 4 minutes, then stir in the garbanzos, tomatoes, and half the stock and bring to the boil. Season to taste with salt and pepper, then simmer for about 20 minutes.
4. Meanwhile, put the rice mix in a separate pan and add twice the volume of cold water and a little salt. Bring to the boil, then cover and simmer over a very low heat for 15 minutes, or as directed on the packet. Some rice mixes may take a little longer.
5. By this time the curry should be rich and thick. If necessary, raise the heat to boil off any extra liquid, or add a little more of the stock or hot water.
6. Serve the curry with naan bread and mango chutney on the side if you like.

Cod in lemon sauce with olives

Cod is a major favorite, but any white fish will work for this recipe. Some of the newly popular varieties, such as pollack, work well. Try to buy fish from sustainable sources to protect the stocks of important species throughout the world.

Serves 4

30g/1oz/2 tbsp butter
1 tbsp oil
3 potatoes, peeled and thickly sliced
4 cod fillets
1 tbsp all-purpose flour
3 zucchini, sliced
100g/4oz/1 cup black olives, pitted
Salt and freshly ground black pepper
Grated zest and juice of 1 lemon
150ml/¼pt/⅔ cup fish stock
6 cherry tomatoes
A few rosemary sprigs

To serve
Boiled long-grain rice

1. Heat the oven to 200°C/400°F/Gas 6. Put the butter and oil in a large baking pan and put in the oven to melt and heat up.
2. Put the potatoes in a saucepan, just cover with lightly salted water and bring to the boil, then drain.
3. Toss the cod fillets in the flour, shaking off any excess. Place in the baking pan, then surround with the zucchini slices and the drained potatoes. Sprinkle with the olives and season with salt and pepper.
4. Whisk the lemon zest and juice into the stock, season with salt and pepper and pour over the fish. Add the tomatoes and cover loosely with foil.
5. Place in the oven for about 30 minutes until cooked through, spooning the sauce over the ingredients once or twice during cooking. Lift off the foil for the last 10 minutes of cooking.
6. Garnish with fresh rosemary sprigs and serve with rice.

Grilled teriyaki salmon with tomatoes

Healthy salmon steaks can be cooked in a matter of minutes. If you plan ahead, you can make the marinade in advance and freeze the salmon steaks in the marinade, so they are ready whenever you only have minutes to make a meal.

Serves 4

For the marinade
2 tbsp teriyaki marinade
2 tbsp honey
1 tbsp balsamic vinegar
1 garlic clove, crushed

For the fish
4 salmon steaks
1 tbsp oil
2 red bell peppers, cut into thick strips

For the salad
8 tomatoes, halved
A few dill sprigs
2 tbsp olive oil
2 tsp lemon juice
1 tsp mustard
1 tsp soft brown sugar (optional)
Salt and freshly ground black pepper
A handful of mixed salad leaves

To serve
Boiled long-grain rice

1. Mix together all the marinade ingredients in a shallow bowl, add the fish and turn in the marinade, then cover and chill overnight, if possible.
2. Lift the fish out of the marinade. Heat the oil in a griddle pan or skillet over a medium-high heat. Add the fish and sauté for about 5 minutes. Turn the fish over, add the bell peppers to the pan with any remaining marinade and continue to cook for a further 6 minutes, spooning the juices over the vegetables and fish.
3. Whisk together the oil, lemon juice, and mustard. Taste and season with sugar, if liked, and salt and pepper. Toss the salad leaves in the dressing.
4. Add the tomatoes to the pan, cut-side down, and turn the heat up high to finish cooking for the final 2 minutes. The skin should be crisp and nicely browned, and the flesh should flake easily when tested with a fork.
5. Arrange the salad on serving plates, sit the salmon and vegetables on top and garnish with the dill sprigs. Serve with boiled rice.

Crispy fish with vegetables

Perfect when you have only minutes to prepare your meal, fish is light and healthy, quick to cook, and very versatile. To make it even quicker, you can use a jar of red bell peppers that have already been roasted. Choose any white fish fillet.

Serves 4

1 egg, lightly beaten
3 tbsp fine oatmeal
Salt and freshly ground black pepper
4 white fish fillets
30g/1oz/2 tbsp butter
1 tbsp olive oil
2 red bell peppers, cut into thin strips
2 zucchini, cut into thin strips with a vegetable peeler
2 tsp fennel seeds
1½ tsp dried lavender flowers

To serve
Boiled new potatoes
Butter

1. Put the egg and oatmeal in separate shallow bowls and season the oatmeal with salt and pepper. Dip the fish in the egg, then in the oatmeal so it is lightly covered.
2. Heat the butter and oil in a large skillet over a medium-high heat, add the fish in the center of the pan and surround with the pepper and zucchini strips. Sprinkle with the fennel seeds and lavender.
3. Sauté for about 5 minutes until the underside of the fish is golden and crisp, then turn it over and brown the other side. Meanwhile, stir the vegetables gently so they are softened but still slightly crunchy.
4. Serve with new potatoes tossed in a little butter.

Chicken thighs with white wine sauce

Deliciously smooth and creamy, the sauce is made with wine and a little crème fraîche and coats a mixture of butter-fried mushrooms. You can use chicken thighs, portions, wings or goujons—or turkey too.

Serves 4

1 tbsp oil
15g/½oz/1 tbsp butter
8 chicken thighs
Salt and freshly ground black pepper
A pinch of paprika
1 tbsp chopped thyme

For the sauce

30g/1oz/2 tbsp butter
1 garlic clove, crushed
225g/8oz mixed chestnut, button or other mushrooms, sliced
2 tbsp all-purpose flour
120ml/4fl oz/½ cup white wine
120ml/4fl oz/½ cup stock
2 tbsp heavy cream

To serve

Mixed salad

1. Heat the oil and butter in a large skillet over a medium-high heat. Season the chicken with salt, pepper, and paprika, add to the pan, and sauté for a few minutes, turning until browned on all sides.
2. Sprinkle with the thyme, turn down the heat, and continue to sauté for about 15 minutes, depending on the thickness of the chicken, until it is cooked through and tender.
3. Meanwhile, to make the sauce, melt the butter in a separate pan, add the garlic and mushrooms, and sauté for about 5 minutes.

The mushrooms will go moist and then the liquid will start to boil off.
4. Whisk in the flour and cook for 1 minute, then add the wine and continue to whisk for 2 minutes. Whisk in the stock and bring to the boil. Turn down the heat and simmer gently until the mushrooms are soft and the sauce is smooth and thick.
5. To finish, remove the sauce from the heat and stir in the heavy cream. Serve the chicken with the mushroom sauce and a mixed salad.

Baked chicken with black beans and rice

A rich and mildly spicy tomato sauce makes this chicken dish a succulent and filling meal to rustle up when time is short. It freezes well, too, making it even more convenient for people in a hurry to enjoy a tasty meal.

Serves 4

1 tbsp oil
1 onion, chopped
1 garlic clove, chopped
1 red bell pepper, chopped
900g/2lb chicken thighs
50g/2oz chorizo, chopped
1 tbsp ground cumin
1 tbsp paprika
A pinch of hot chilli powder
400g/14oz/1 large can chopped tomatoes
2 tbsp tomato paste
120ml/4fl oz/½ cup chicken stock
400g/14oz/1 large can red kidney beans, rinsed and drained
1 tbsp chopped cilantro
Salt and freshly ground black pepper
4 tomatoes, cut into chunks
A few basil leaves

To serve
Boiled long-grain rice

1. Heat the oven to 180°C/350°F/Gas 4.
2. Heat the oil in a flameproof Dutch oven and sauté the onion, garlic, and pepper for a few minutes over a medium heat until softened.
3. Add the chicken and sauté until browned.
4. Add the chorizo, then sprinkle with the spices and keep stirring so that the chicken is coated in the spiced oil.
5. Add the tomatoes, tomato paste, and stock, and bring to the boil. Stir in the beans and cilantro and season with salt and pepper. Cover and cook in the oven for 30 minutes until the chicken is tender and the sauce has reduced. If you prefer a thicker sauce, return the Dutch oven to the hob and cook over a medium heat, uncovered, until thickened to your liking.
6. Garnish with tomatoes and basil and serve with boiled rice.

Serves 4

450g/1lb chicken breasts, cut into cubes

6 tomatoes, cut into wedges

1 red bell pepper, cut into chunks

3 zucchini, sliced

1 onion, cut into wedges

2 tbsp oil

2 tbsp chopped parsley

Salt and freshly ground black pepper

To serve

New or jacket potatoes

Grated carrot salad

Chicken and pepper kebabs

Whether cooked under the broiler or on the barbecue, kebabs can be served on their own as an appetizer, with salad as a light lunch, or with vegetables and rice, pasta, or baked potatoes to make a quick and delicious meal.

1. Soak some wooden skewers in water for at least 30 minutes.
2. Thread the chicken, tomatoes, pepper, zucchini, and onion alternately on to the skewers. Brush with oil and season with salt and pepper.
3. Place under a hot broiler for about 15 minutes, turning regularly and brushing with a little more oil if necessary, until the chicken is tender.
4. Sprinkle with parsley and serve with new or jacket potatoes and a carrot salad.

A quick dip in a herb and spice marinade helps to flavor and tenderize pork chops so they cook beautifully and give tasty results. Simple and elegant, this meal only requires some fresh and colorful green vegetables to make it complete.

Spiced pork chops with sweet potato mash

Serves 4

4 pork chops

450g/1lb sweet potatoes, peeled and cut into chunks

Salt and freshly ground black pepper

200g/7oz green beans, trimmed

30g/1oz/2 tbsp butter

2 tbsp milk

For the marinade

4 tbsp olive oil

4 tbsp white wine vinegar

3 tbsp Dijon mustard

1 garlic clove, crushed

2 tbsp chopped sage

1 bay leaf

1. Mix together all the marinade ingredients. Pour over the pork chops, cover and leave in the fridge to marinate for 30 minutes, or longer if possible. If you can leave them overnight, that's great.

2. You can broil or barbecue the chops. Lift them out of the marinade and put in a hot griddle pan, under a hot broiler or over barbecue coals. Cook for about 20 minutes until tender and cooked to your liking, turning occasionally. Baste with the marinade from time to time.

3. Meanwhile, put the sweet potatoes in a pan, just cover with water and add a little salt. Bring to the boil, cover, and simmer gently for about 20 minutes until tender.

4. At the same time, bring a separate pan of lightly salted water to the boil, add the beans and return to the boil for about 5 minutes until just tender but still with a bit of crunch.

5. Drain the sweet potatoes and mash with the butter and milk until smooth. Season with salt and pepper. Drain the beans.

6. Serve the chops with the sweet potatoes and beans.

Serves 4

300g/12oz fine rice noodles

1 tbsp oil

200g/7oz pork fillets or chicken, cut into strips

1 onion, thinly sliced

1 red bell pepper, cut into strips

2 garlic cloves, crushed

2cm/1in piece of root ginger

2 zucchini, thinly sliced

2 tsp five-spice powder

1 tsp turmeric

60ml/2fl oz/4 tbsp dark soy sauce

2 tbsp lime juice

4 scallions, sliced into rings

60ml/2fl oz/4 tbsp chicken stock

1 tbsp sesame seeds

Bringing a little Chinese style to your kitchen, chunks of pork or chicken nestle among scallions, zucchini, and bell peppers on a bed of noodles tossed with a rich sauce and sprinkled with sesame seeds.

Stir-fried pork with noodles

1. Soak the noodles according to the packet directions, then drain.
2. Heat the oil in a wok over a medium heat and sauté the pork or chicken until browned. Remove from the pan.
3. Add the onion, pepper, garlic, and ginger, and sauté for a few minutes until softened.
4. Add the zucchini, then stir in the spices, soy sauce, lime juice, scallions, and stock.
5. Drain the noodles and add them to the pan with the pork, raising the heat to high. Toss all the ingredients together until hot and well blended, then serve sprinkled with sesame seeds.

Baked potatoes with hot beef chili

If you have time, this tastes best if it is simmered for up to an hour. If time is really short, you can serve it in 30 minutes by starting the potatoes in the microwave for about 7 minutes before putting them in the oven for 20 minutes.

1. Heat the oven to 200°C/400°F/Gas 6.
2. Prick the skins of the potatoes with a fork and put them in the oven for about 1 hour, depending on size, until you can squeeze them gently but the skins are crisp.
3. Meanwhile, heat the oil in a large pan over a medium heat and sauté the onions, garlic, chili, carrot, and peppers for 5 minutes until soft but not browned.
4. Add the mushrooms and sauté until softened and blended.
5. Stir in the beef and continue to cook for about 5 minutes until browned and the grains are separate.
6. Add the wine and boil for 1 minute, then add the tomatoes and sieved tomatoes and bring to the boil. Add some chili powder, if liked, and season with salt and pepper. Stir in the beans. Simmer gently for at least 20 minutes until thickened and well blended. Ideally, leave to simmer for 1 hour.
7. When ready to serve, cut a cross in each potato and mash a little butter into the flesh. Spoon the chili on top and serve.

Serves 4

4 large baking potatoes
2 tbsp oil
2 onions, chopped
2 garlic cloves, chopped
1 red chili, deseeded and chopped
1 carrot, chopped
2 bell peppers, red and green, chopped
100g/4oz mushrooms, chopped
500g/1lb 2oz ground beef
100ml/3½fl oz/scant ½ cup red wine
400g/14oz/1 large can chopped tomatoes
200g/7oz/1 small can sieved tomatoes
1–2 tsp chili powder (optional)
Salt and freshly ground black pepper
400g/14oz/1 large can red kidney beans, drained
50g/2oz/¼ cup butter

Who said sandwiches are dull? Put the fun back into this quick meal just by adding a few well-chosen ingredients and presenting them with a little imagination. If you think it's a tall order to come up with new lunchtime ideas, this could be your answer!

Skyscraper sandwiches

Serves 4

8 large slices of various breads, such as wholemeal, granary, ciabatta, cottage loaf
75g/3oz/⅓ cup butter
Salt and freshly ground black pepper

For a paprika chicken filling
1 tsp oil
1 small garlic clove
1 chicken breast, cut into strips
1 tsp paprika or cayenne
½ red bell pepper, cut into strips
½ yellow bell pepper, cut into strips
A small handful of arugula leaves
A small handful of flatleaf parsley
1 tsp red pepper pesto sauce
1 tbsp soured cream or mayonnaise

For a bacon and salami filling
2 bacon slices
4 slices of salami
50g/2oz goats' cheese, diced
2 tomatoes, sliced
A small handful of mixed salad leaves
2 tbsp mayonnaise

1. You can use one type of bread or several to offer a variety of sandwiches or make them all the same—the choice is up to you. With these ingredients, you can make 4 large sandwiches with 2 different fillings. Serve them hot or cold, cut in half, or made with 16 slices of small loaves—or anything that suits you.

2. Choose 8 large slices of bread either in pairs or mixing different breads in the same sandwich, making sure they are of a similar size and shape.

3. Broil the bread so it is toasted how you like it on both sides, then spread with a little butter.

4. For a paprika chicken and pepper sandwich, heat the oil in a small skillet over a medium heat and add the garlic clove. Sprinkle the chicken with the paprika and season with salt and pepper. Sauté for about 10 minutes until cooked through and golden brown on the outside.

5. Meanwhile, for a bacon and salami sandwich, sauté the bacon in a pan over a medium heat for about 10 minutes until cooked through and crisped to your liking. Alternatively, you can broil the bacon.

6. Arrange the cooked chicken on 2 slices of bread and top with the peppers, arugula, and parsley. Mix the pesto into the soured cream and spread over the second slice, then place it on top.

7. Arrange the bacon on another 2 slices and top with the salami, goats' cheese, tomatoes, and salad leaves, then dot with mayonnaise and season with a little salt and plenty of pepper. Top with the remaining bread.

8. Stack the sandwiches in a tall pile and serve with panache!

Makes 12

225g/8oz/2 cups all-purpose flour

1 tsp baking powder

100g/4oz/½ cup superfine sugar

250ml/8fl oz/1 cup milk

120ml/4fl oz/½ cup sunflower oil

1 egg, lightly beaten

150g/5oz/1 cup chopped mixed fruits, such as raspberries, redcurrants, blackberries and strawberries

1 tsp confectioners' sugar

1 tsp shredded coconut

Red berry muffins

For a snack or a dessert, with morning coffee or even for breakfast, muffins are so versatile that they should be part of everyone's culinary repertoire. Here, the red berries melt into the muffins to give a gorgeous result.

1. Heat the oven to 200°C/400°F/Gas 6 and line a muffin pan with paper cases.
2. Mix the flour, baking powder, and sugar in a bowl and make a well in the center.
3. Measure the milk and oil into a measuring jug and add the egg. Pour into the dry ingredients and stir and fold together quickly until the dry ingredients are just incorporated. Don't overmix or the muffins will be tough.
4. Gently fold in the fruit, then spoon the mixture into the paper cases.
5. Bake in the oven for about 20 minutes until well risen, golden on top, and slightly springy to the touch.
6. Transfer to a wire rack to cool. Put the sugar and shredded coconut in a sieve and rub through the sieve over the top of the muffins.

Bakewell tarts

A classic English dessert, these almond-flavored cakes can be made as individual servings or as one round or square tart to cut into slices or squares. They are delicious cold served with cream, or try them warm with lashings of custard.

Serves 4

For the base

75g/3oz/⅓ cup butter

175g/6oz/1½ cups plain flour

2 tbsp sugar

I egg yolk

2 tbsp water

For the filling

150g/5oz/⅔ cup butter

150g/5oz/⅔ cup superfine sugar

150g/5oz/1½ cups ground almonds

Grated zest of 1 lemon

3 eggs, lightly beaten

3 tbsp raspberry jam

25g/1oz/¼ cup slivered almonds

1. Heat the oven to 180°C/350°F/Gas 4 and grease and line a 12-hole cake tin.
2. Rub the butter into the flour until the mixture resembles breadcrumbs. Stir in the sugar. Stir in the egg yolk, then gradually add enough of the water to mix to a soft dough. Wrap in plastic wrap and chill for 1 hour.
3. Roll out the dough on a lightly floured surface and use to line the prepared tins. Prick the bases with a fork. Cover with baking paper, fill with baking beans and bake in the oven for 10 minutes. Remove the paper and beans and return to the oven for a further 2 minutes.
4. Beat the butter and sugar together until light and creamy. Stir in the ground almonds and lemon zest, then beat in the eggs.
5. Spread the jam over the base of the pastry cases, then spoon in the almond mixture. Bake in the oven for 15 minutes.
6. Sprinkle with the slivered almonds and return to the oven for a further 5 minutes until the filling is set and the top is golden.

Oat, rhubarb, and apple crumble

Whatever fruits you include beneath your crumble base, you will be sure to create a delicious dessert that is so quick to put together. You could even use a pie filling, which means you can make it in even fewer minutes.

Serves 4

200g/7oz rhubarb, cut into chunks

450g/1lb dessert apples, peeled, cored and coarsely chopped

1 tsp ground cinnamon

1 tsp clear honey

75g/3oz/⅓ cup butter

For the topping

150g/5oz/1¼ cups all-purpose flour

A pinch of ground ginger

75g/3oz/⅓ cup butter

50g/2oz/½ cup oatmeal or rolled oats

50g/2oz/¼ cup demerara sugar

To serve

A thyme sprig

Cream or custard

1. Heat the oven to 180°C/350°F/ Gas 4 and grease an ovenproof dish.
2. Rinse the fruit, then put it into the prepared dish with just the water clinging to it. Sprinkle with cinnamon, drizzle with honey, and dot with butter.
3. For the topping, mix the flour and ginger. Rub in the butter until the mixture resembles breadcrumbs. Stir in the oatmeal and sugar.
4. Sprinkle the crumble over the fruit and bake in the oven for 35 minutes until the fruit is just soft and the topping is golden and crisp.
5. Garnish with the thyme and serve with cream or custard.